2023

Gooseberry Patch

An imprint of Globe Pequot
246 Goose Lane
Guilford, CT 06437

www.gooseberrypatch.com
1•800•854•6673

Copyright 2022, Gooseberry Patch 978-1-62093-467-8

Your recipe could appear in our next cookbook!

Share your tried & true family favorite recipes with us instantly at

www.gooseberrypatch.com

If you'd rather jot 'em down by hand, send them to us at:

Gooseberry Patch
Attn: Cookbook Dept.
PO Box 812
Columbus, OH 43216-0812

Don't forget to include the number of servings your recipe makes, plus your name, address, phone number and email address. If we select your recipe, your name will appear right along with it and you'll receive a **FREE** copy of the cookbook!

January

January

Notes

Sunday	Monday	Tuesday
1 New Year's Day	2	3
8	9	10
15	16 Martin Luther King, Jr. Day	17
22	23	24
29	30	31

December

S	M	T	W	T	F	S
					1	2	3
4	5	6	7	8	9	10
11	12	13	14	15	16	17
18	19	20	21	22	23	24
25	26	27	28	29	30	31

February

S	M	T	W	T	F	S
			1	2	3	4
5	6	7	8	9	10	11
12	13	14	15	16	17	18
19	20	21	22	23	24	25
26	27	28				

2023

Wednesday	Thursday	Friday	Saturday
4	5	6	7
11	12	13	14
18	19	20	21
25	26	27	28

January

Snow Day Play Clay

1/3 c. margarine, softened
1/3 c. corn syrup
1/4 t. salt
1 t. vanilla extract
16-oz. pkg. powdered sugar
assorted food coloring

Combine margarine, corn syrup, salt and vanilla extract in a
mixing bowl; mix well. Add powdered sugar a little at a time,
mixing with your hands; add additional corn syrup if mixture
is too dry. Divide clay into smaller parts and add a few drops
of food coloring to make different colors. Store in refrigerator
in airtight containers. Makes 2 cups.

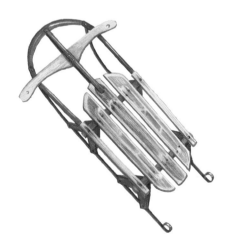

1 Sunday

January

Monday **2**

Tuesday **3**

Wednesday **4**

Thursday **5**

Friday **6**

Saturday **7**

Sunday **8**

January

9 Monday

10 Tuesday

11 Wednesday

12 Thursday

13 Friday

14 Saturday

15 Sunday

January

Martin Luther King, Jr. Day _____ *Monday* **16**

_____ *Tuesday* **17**

_____ *Wednesday* **18**

_____ *Thursday* **19**

_____ *Friday* **20**

_____ *Saturday* **21**

_____ *Sunday* **22**

January

23 Monday

24 Tuesday

25 Wednesday

26 Thursday

27 Friday

28 Saturday

29 Sunday

January

Monday 30

Tuesday 31

The leaves fall, the wind blows, and the farm country slowly changes from the summer cottons into its winter wools.

-Henry Beston

Cranberry-Pecan Coffee Cakes

1/2 c. butter, softened
1 c. sugar
2 eggs
2 c. all-purpose flour
2 t. baking powder
1/2 t. baking soda
1/2 t. salt

8-oz. container sour cream
1 t. almond extract
1 t. vanilla extract
16-oz. can whole-berry
   cranberry sauce
1 c. coarsely chopped pecans

Beat butter at medium speed with an electric mixer until creamy.
Gradually add sugar, beating well. Add eggs, one at a time,
beating until blended after each addition. Combine flour and next
3 ingredients. Add flour mixture to butter mixture alternately
with sour cream, beginning and ending with flour mixture. Stir in
extracts. Spoon 1/2 cup batter into each of 4 greased and floured
5"x3" mini loaf pans. Gently stir cranberry sauce; spoon 3
tablespoons over batter in each pan and spread lightly to edges.
Sprinkle 2 tablespoons pecans over cranberry sauce in each pan.
Repeat layers in each pan using remaining batter, cranberry
sauce and pecans. Bake at 350 degrees for 48 to 50 minutes or
until a toothpick inserted in center comes out clean. Cool in pans
on a wire rack 15 minutes; remove from pans and let cool
completely. Drizzle Almond Cream Glaze over cooled cakes.
Makes 4 mini coffee cakes.

Almond Cream Glaze:

3/4 c. powdered sugar
2 T. whipping cream

1/2 t. almond extract

Stir together all ingredients. Makes 1/3 cup.

I Love U!

February

February

Notes

Sunday	Monday	Tuesday
5	6	7
12	13	14 Valentine's Day
19	20 Presidents' Day	21
26	27	28

January

S	M	T	W	T	F	S
1	2	3	4	5	6	7
8	9	10	11	12	13	14
15	16	17	18	19	20	21
22	23	24	25	26	27	28
29	30	31				

March

S	M	T	W	T	F	S
			1	2	3	4
5	6	7	8	9	10	11
12	13	14	15	16	17	18
19	20	21	22	23	24	25
26	27	28	29	30	31	

2023

Wednesday	Thursday	Friday	Saturday
1	2 Groundhog Day	3	4
8	9	10	11
15	16	17	18
22 Ash Wednesday	23	24	25

Love at first sight is easy to understand; it's when two people have been looking at each other for a lifetime that it becomes a miracle.

—Amy Bloom

February

Bring out the kid in everyone with a decorate-your-own cupcake station. Serve vanilla and chocolate cupcakes on cake stands, along with assorted tinted frostings and fun toppings.

1 Wednesday

2 Thursday   Groundhog Day

3 Friday

4 Saturday

5 Sunday

February

Monday 6

Tuesday 7

Wednesday 8

Thursday 9

Friday 10

Saturday 11

Sunday 12

February

13 Monday _____

14 Tuesday _____ <small>Valentine's Day</small>

15 Wednesday _____

16 Thursday _____

17 Friday _____

18 Saturday _____

19 Sunday _____

February

Presidents' Day   _Monday_ **20**

Tuesday **21**

Ash Wednesday   _Wednesday_ **22**

Thursday **23**

Friday **24**

Saturday **25**

Sunday **26**

February

27 Monday

28 Tuesday

Sweetheart Shakes

3 c. milk, divided
1 c. vanilla ice cream,
  softened
3-1/2 oz. pkg. instant vanilla
  pudding mix, divided

1 c. strawberry ice cream,
  softened
3 drops red food coloring

Pour 1-1/2 cups milk into a blender; add vanilla ice cream and
1/3 of dry pudding mix. Cover; blend on high until smooth,
about 15 seconds. Pour into 4 freezer-safe glasses; freeze for
30 minutes. Combine remaining milk, pudding mix, strawberry
ice cream and food coloring in blender; cover and blend until
smooth, about 15 seconds. Pour into glasses on top of vanilla
portion and serve. Serves 4.

March

March

Sunday	Monday	Tuesday
5	6	7
12 Daylight Savings Begins	13 Commonwealth Day (Canada)	14
19	20 First Day of Spring	21
26	27	28

February

S	M	T	W	T	F	S
			1	2	3	4
5	6	7	8	9	10	11
12	13	14	15	16	17	18
19	20	21	22	23	24	25
26	27	28				

April

S	M	T	W	T	F	S
						1
2	3	4	5	6	7	8
9	10	11	12	13	14	15
16	17	18	19	20	21	22
23/30	24	25	26	27	28	29

2023

Wednesday	Thursday	Friday	Saturday
1	2	3	4
8	9	10	11
15	16	17 St. Patrick's Day	18
22	23	24	25
29	30	31	

March

Make-Ahead French Toast

1 loaf French, Italian, challah
   or Hawaiian bread, cut
   into 1-inch slices
3 eggs, beaten
1-1/2 c. milk
1 c. half-and-half

1/2 c. egg substitute
1 T. pumpkin pie spice
1 t. vanilla extract
1/4 t. salt
1/2 c. brown sugar, packed
1 to 2 T. butter, sliced

Arrange bread slices in bottom of a greased 13"x9" baking pan.
Whisk together eggs, milk, half-and-half, egg substitute, spice,
vanilla and salt. Stir in brown sugar; pour mixture over bread
slices. Refrigerate, covered, overnight. Dot top with butter and
bake, uncovered, at 350 degrees for 40 to 45 minutes. Makes
8 servings.

1 Wednesday

2 Thursday

3 Friday

4 Saturday

5 Sunday

March

Monday 6

Tuesday 7

Wednesday 8

Thursday 9

Friday 10

Saturday 11

Daylight Savings Begins

Sunday 12

March

13 _Monday_ Commonwealth Day
(Canada)

14 Tuesday

15 Wednesday

16 Thursday

17 Friday   St. Patrick's Day

18 Saturday

19 Sunday

March

First Day of Spring

Monday 20

Tuesday 21

Wednesday 22

Thursday 23

Friday 24

Saturday 25

Sunday 26

March

27 Monday

28 Tuesday

29 Wednesday

30 Thursday

31 Friday

April

April

Sunday	Monday	Tuesday

I'm youth, I'm joy, I'm a little bird that has broken out of the egg.

- James M. Barrie

Sunday	Monday	Tuesday
2 Palm Sunday	3	4
9 Easter	10 Easter Monday (Canada)	11
16	17	18
23 / 30	24	25

March
S	M	T	W	T	F	S
			1	2	3	4
5	6	7	8	9	10	11
12	13	14	15	16	17	18
19	20	21	22	23	24	25
26	27	28	29	30	31	

May
S	M	T	W	T	F	S
	1	2	3	4	5	6
7	8	9	10	11	12	13
14	15	16	17	18	19	20
21	22	23	24	25	26	27
28	29	30	31			

2023

Wednesday	Thursday	Friday	Saturday
			1 April Fool's Day
5 Passover (Sundown)	6	7 Good Friday	8
12	13	14	15
19	20	21	22
26	27	28	29

April

Lizzy's Make-Ahead Egg Casserole

1 doz. eggs, beaten
1 c. cooked ham, diced
3 c. whole milk

12 frozen waffles, divided
2 c. shredded Cheddar
  cheese, divided

In a large bowl, beat eggs. Stir in ham and milk. Grease a 13"x9" baking pan. Place one layer of waffles in the bottom of the pan. Pour half of the mixture on the waffles. Sprinkle with half of the cheese. Continue layering waffles, egg mixture and cheese. Cover and refrigerate overnight. Uncover and bake at 350 degrees for about one hour or until eggs are set. Serves 12.

1 Saturday

April Fool's Day

2 Sunday

Palm Sunday

April

Monday 3

Tuesday 4

Passover (Sundown) Wednesday 5

Thursday 6

Good Friday Friday 7

Saturday 8

Easter Sunday 9

April

10 Monday   Easter Monday (Canada)

11 Tuesday

12 Wednesday

13 Thursday

14 Friday

15 Saturday

16 Sunday

April

Monday 17

Tuesday 18

Wednesday 19

Thursday 20

Friday 21

Saturday 22

Sunday 23

April

24 _Monday_ _____

25 _Tuesday_ _____

26 _Wednesday_ _____

27 _Thursday_ _____

28 _Friday_ _____

29 _Saturday_ _____

30 _Sunday_ _____

May

May

Sunday	Monday	Tuesday
	1 May Day	2
7	8	9
14 Mothers' Day	15	16
21	22 Victoria Day (Canada)	23
28	29 Memorial Day	30

April

S	M	T	W	T	F	S
						1
2	3	4	5	6	7	8
9	10	11	12	13	14	15
16	17	18	19	20	21	22
23/30	24	25	26	27	28	29

June

S	M	T	W	T	F	S
				1	2	3
4	5	6	7	8	9	10
11	12	13	14	15	16	17
18	19	20	21	22	23	24
25	26	27	28	29	30	

2023

Wednesday	Thursday	Friday	Saturday
3	4	5	6
10	11	12	13
17	18	19	20
24	25	26	27
31			

A mother is she who can take the
place of all others but whose place
no one else can take.

— Cardinal Mermillod

May

1 Monday   May Day

2 Tuesday

3 Wednesday

4 Thursday

5 Friday

6 Saturday

7 Sunday

May

Monday 8

Tuesday 9

Wednesday 10

Thursday 11

Friday 12

Saturday 13

Mothers' Day   Sunday 14

May

15 Monday

16 Tuesday

17 Wednesday

18 Thursday

19 Friday

20 Saturday

21 Sunday

May

Victoria Day (Canada)

Monday 22

Tuesday 23

Wednesday 24

Thursday 25

Friday 26

Saturday 27

Sunday 28

May

Fresh Fruit Kabobs & Poppy Seed Dip

6 c. fresh fruit like strawberries, kiwi, pineapple,
    honeydew and cantaloupe, peeled and cut into
    bite-size cubes or slices
8 to 10 wooden skewers

Arrange fruit pieces alternately on skewers. Serve Poppy Seed
Dip alongside fruit kabobs. Makes 8 to 10 servings.

Poppy Seed Dip:

1 c. vanilla yogurt   1 t. vanilla extract
2 T. honey   1 t. poppy seed
4 t. lime juice

Stir together ingredients in a small bowl.
Keep chilled.

June

June

Notes

Sunday	Monday	Tuesday

In the morning, very early, that's the time I love to go barefoot where the fern grows curly and grass is cool between each toe. On a summer morning-O! On a summer morning.

— Rachel Field

Sunday	Monday	Tuesday
4	5	6
11	12	13
18	19	20
Fathers' Day	Juneteenth	
25	26	27

May

S	M	T	W	T	F	S
	1	2	3	4	5	6
7	8	9	10	11	12	13
14	15	16	17	18	19	20
21	22	23	24	25	26	27
28	29	30	31			

July

S	M	T	W	T	F	S
						1
2	3	4	5	6	7	8
9	10	11	12	13	14	15
16	17	18	19	20	21	22
23/30	24/31	25	26	27	28	29

2023

Wednesday	Thursday	Friday	Saturday
	1	2	3
7	8	9	10
14	15	16	17
Flag Day			
21	22	23	24
First Day of Summer			
28	29	30	

June

Beverly's Bacon Burgers

1-1/2 lbs. ground beef
1 baking potato, peeled
   and diced
2 carrots, peeled and grated
1/2 onion, grated
1 egg, beaten

1 t. dried parsley
3/4 t. garlic, minced
1/2 t. salt
pepper to taste
6 to 7 slices bacon
6 to 7 sandwich buns, split

In a large bowl, combine all ingredients except bacon and buns. Mix well; form into 6 to 7 patties. Wrap a bacon slice around each patty and secure with a wooden toothpick. Grill over medium heat to desired doneness. Serve on buns. Makes 6 to 7 servings.

1   Thursday

2   Friday

3   Saturday

4   Sunday

June

Monday 5

Tuesday 6

Wednesday 7

Thursday 8

Friday 9

Saturday 10

Sunday 11

June

12 Monday _____

13 Tuesday _____

14 Wednesday _____ Flag Day

15 Thursday _____

16 Friday _____

17 Saturday _____

18 Sunday _____ Fathers' Day

June

Juneteenth   *Monday* 19

Tuesday 20

First Day of Summer   *Wednesday* 21

Thursday 22

Friday 23

Saturday 24

Sunday 25

June

26 Monday

27 Tuesday

28 Wednesday

29 Thursday

30 Friday

July

July

Sunday	Monday	Tuesday

What is patriotism but the love of the good things we ate in our childhood?

-Lin Yutang

2	3	4
		Independence Day
9	10	11
16	17	18
23 / 30	24 / 31	25

June
S	M	T	W	T	F	S
					1	2	3
4	5	6	7	8	9	10
11	12	13	14	15	16	17
18	19	20	21	22	23	24
25	26	27	28	29	30

August
S	M	T	W	T	F	S
		1	2	3	4	5
6	7	8	9	10	11	12
13	14	15	16	17	18	19
20	21	22	23	24	25	26
27	28	29	30	31

2023

Wednesday	Thursday	Friday	Saturday
			1 Canada Day (Canada)
5	6	7	8
12	13	14	15
19	20	21	22
26	27	28	29

July

Iced Cowboy Coffee

5 c. milk
2 T. instant coffee powder
1 whole nutmeg, finely
   grated

1 sq. sweet baking
   chocolate, grated
2 T. brown sugar, packed
ice cubes

In a saucepan, whisk together milk, coffee, nutmeg,
chocolate and sugar until heated through. When chocolate
has melted mix thoroughly. Serve over ice. Makes 4 to
6 servings.

1 Saturday   Canada Day
                                                    (Canada)

2 Sunday

July

_____ Monday 3

Independence Day _____ Tuesday 4

_____ Wednesday 5

_____ Thursday 6

_____ Friday 7

_____ Saturday 8

_____ Sunday 9

July

10 Monday _____

11 Tuesday _____

12 Wednesday _____

13 Thursday _____

14 Friday _____

15 Saturday _____

16 Sunday _____

July

Monday 17

Tuesday 18

Wednesday 19

Thursday 20

Friday 21

Saturday 22

Sunday 23

July

24 Monday

25 Tuesday

26 Wednesday

27 Thursday

28 Friday

29 Saturday

30 Sunday

July

Simple pleasures at this time of
year are best when enjoyed on
the front porch swing. Whip up a
pitcher of lemonade or mint iced
tea, add a few fluffy pillows and
throw in a good book...there's just
no better way to enjoy the day.

July

Patriotic Cupcakes

2 c. sugar
1 c. butter, softened
2 eggs
2 t. lemon juice
1 t. vanilla extract
2-1/2 c. cake flour

1/2 t. baking soda
1 c. buttermilk
Garnish: 16-oz. can white
  frosting; red, white and
  blue sprinkles

Beat sugar and butter at medium speed with an electric mixer until creamy. Add eggs, one at a time, beating until yellow disappears after each addition. Beat in lemon juice and vanilla. Combine flour and baking soda in a small bowl; add to sugar mixture alternately with buttermilk, beginning and ending with flour mixture. Beat at medium speed just until blended after each addition. Spoon batter into paper-lined muffin cups, filling 2/3 full. Bake at 350 degrees for 18 to 22 minutes or until a toothpick inserted in center comes out clean. Cool in pans on a wire rack 10 minutes. Remove cupcakes from pans to wire rack; cool 45 minutes or until completely cool. Spread frosting on cupcakes. Immediately decorate with desired red, white and blue sprinkles. Place cupcakes on plate in a flag pattern. Makes 2 dozen.

August

August

Sunday	Monday	Tuesday
		1
6	7	8
13	14	15
20	21	22
27	28	29

July

S	M	T	W	T	F	S
						1
2	3	4	5	6	7	8
9	10	11	12	13	14	15
16	17	18	19	20	21	22
23/30	24/31	25	26	27	28	29

September

S	M	T	W	T	F	S
					1	2
3	4	5	6	7	8	9
10	11	12	13	14	15	16
17	18	19	20	21	22	23
24	25	26	27	28	29	30

2023

Wednesday	Thursday	Friday	Saturday
2	3	4	5
9	10	11	12
16	17	18	19
23	24	25	26
30	31		

August

Dining outdoors on a hot, humid day? Keep salt free-flowing...simply add a few grains of rice to the shaker.

1 Tuesday

2 Wednesday

3 Thursday

4 Friday

5 Saturday

6 Sunday

August

Monday 7

Tuesday 8

Wednesday 9

Thursday 10

Friday 11

Saturday 12

Sunday 13

August

14 Monday

15 Tuesday

16 Wednesday

17 Thursday

18 Friday

19 Saturday

20 Sunday

August

Monday 21

Tuesday 22

Wednesday 23

Thursday 24

Friday 25

Saturday 26

Sunday 27

August

28 _Monday_

29 Tuesday

30 Wednesday

31 Thursday

Smoky Grilled Corn

Jazz up some sweet corn! You'll find smoked paprika in the grocery's spice aisle.

8 ears sweet corn, husked
4 T. olive oil, divided
1 T. kosher salt, divided
1 T. pepper, divided
1 T. smoked paprika, divided

Divide corn between 2 large plastic zipping bags. To each bag, add 2 tablespoons oil, 1/2 tablespoon salt, 1/2 tablespoon pepper and 1/2 tablespoon paprika. Close bags and gently toss to coat corn. Remove corn from bags; arrange on a grill over medium-high heat. Grill, turning often, until lightly golden, about 25 minutes. Makes 8 servings.

September

September

Notes

Sunday	Monday	Tuesday

Keep a warm quilt or blanket-stitched throw in the car for autumn picnics and football games...perfect for keeping warm & cozy!

Sunday	Monday	Tuesday
3	4 Labor Day	5
10 Grandparents' Day	11 Patriot Day	12
17	18	19
24 Yom Kippur (Sundown)	25	26

August

S	M	T	W	T	F	S
		1	2	3	4	5
6	7	8	9	10	11	12
13	14	15	16	17	18	19
20	21	22	23	24	25	26
27	28	29	30	31		

October

S	M	T	W	T	F	S
1	2	3	4	5	6	7
8	9	10	11	12	13	14
15	16	17	18	19	20	21
22	23	24	25	26	27	28
29	30	31				

2023

Wednesday	Thursday	Friday	Saturday
		1	2
6	7	8	9
13	14	15 Rosh Hashana (Sundown)	16
20	21	22	23 First Day of Autumn
27	28	29	30

September

So-Good Turkey Burgers

1 lb. ground turkey
2 T. fresh chives, chopped
1/2 c. Italian-flavored dry
   bread crumbs
1/4 c. Worcestershire sauce

1/2 t. dry mustard
salt and pepper to taste
4 to 6 hamburger buns,
   split

Combine all ingredients except buns; form into 4 to 6 patties.
Grill to desired doneness; serve on hamburger buns. Makes
4 to 6 sandwiches.

1   Friday

2   Saturday

3   Sunday

September

_____ *Monday* 4

_____ *Tuesday* 5

_____ *Wednesday* 6

_____ *Thursday* 7

_____ *Friday* 8

_____ *Saturday* 9

Grandparents' Day _____ *Sunday* 10

September

11 Monday   Patriot Day

12 Tuesday

13 Wednesday

14 Thursday

15 Friday   Rosh Hashana (Sundown)

16 Saturday

17 Sunday

September

Monday 18

Tuesday 19

Wednesday 20

Thursday 21

Friday 22

First Day of Autumn

Saturday 23

Yom Kippur (Sundown)

Sunday 24

September

25 Monday

26 Tuesday

27 Wednesday

28 Thursday

29 Friday

30 Saturday

October

October

Notes

Sunday	Monday	Tuesday
1	2	3
8	9 Columbus Day Thanksgiving (Canada)	10
15	16	17
22	23	24
29	30	31 Halloween

September

S	M	T	W	T	F	S
					1	2
3	4	5	6	7	8	9
10	11	12	13	14	15	16
17	18	19	20	21	22	23
24	25	26	27	28	29	30

November

S	M	T	W	T	F	S
			1	2	3	4
5	6	7	8	9	10	11
12	13	14	15	16	17	18
19	20	21	22	23	24	25
26	27	28	29	30		

2023

Wednesday	Thursday	Friday	Saturday
4	5	6	7
11	12	13	14
18	19	20	21 Sweetest Day
25	26	27	28

October gave a party;
The leaves by hundreds came...
The Chestnuts, Oaks, and Maples,
And leaves of every name.

– George Cooper

October

Witches' Brooms

1 c. butter, softened
2 c. brown sugar, packed
2 eggs, beaten
4-1/2 c. all-purpose flour
2 t. baking powder
1 t. baking soda

1/2 c. milk
1 t. vanilla extract
1 t. lemon extract
pretzel rods
Garnish: orange sugar

In a large bowl, combine all ingredients except pretzels and garnish; mix well. Cover; refrigerate for one hour. Roll out dough 1/2-inch thick on a floured surface. Cut out triangle shapes. Place on greased and floured baking sheet with pretzel rod tucked underneath. Add strip of dough at top of triangle. Use a fork to score bottom of triangle. Sprinkle with orange sugar. Bake at 350 degrees for 10 minutes, or until golden around edges. Cool for one minute before removing from baking sheets; cool completely on wax paper. Makes about 4 dozen.

1 Sunday

October

_____ Monday 2

_____ Tuesday 3

_____ Wednesday 4

_____ Thursday 5

_____ Friday 6

_____ Saturday 7

_____ Sunday 8

October

9 *Monday*

Columbus Day
Thanksgiving (Canada)

10 Tuesday

11 Wednesday

12 Thursday

13 Friday

14 Saturday

15 Sunday

October

Monday 16

Tuesday 17

Wednesday 18

Thursday 19

Friday 20

Sweetest Day

Saturday 21

Sunday 22

October

23 Monday

24 Tuesday

25 Wednesday

26 Thursday

27 Friday

28 Saturday

29 Sunday

October

Monday **30**

Tuesday **31**

Halloween

For a special dinner in the fall, line your porch steps with sweet-smelling citronella candles. Get out your plaid stadium blanket and enjoy a midnight dinner on the porch amongst the glow of sparkling carved pumpkins.

October

3-Cheese Pasta Bake

8-oz. pkg. pasta, uncooked
2 T. butter
2 T. all-purpose flour
1-1/2 c. milk
1/2 c. half-and-half
1 c. shredded white
   Cheddar cheese

1/4 c. grated Parmesan
   cheese
2 c. shredded Gruyère
   cheese, divided
1 t. salt
1/4 t. pepper
1/8 t. nutmeg

Prepare pasta according to package directions. Meanwhile, melt butter in a saucepan over medium heat. Whisk in flour until smooth; cook, whisking constantly, one minute. Gradually whisk in milk and half-and-half; cook, whisking constantly, 3 to 5 minutes or until thickened. Stir in Cheddar cheese, Parmesan cheese, one cup Gruyère cheese and next 3 ingredients until smooth. Stir together pasta and cheese mixture; pour into a lightly greased 11"x7" baking pan. Top with remaining Gruyère cheese. Bake, uncovered, at 350 degrees for 15 minutes or until golden and bubbly. Serves 4.

November

November

Notes

Sunday	Monday	Tuesday

Autumn is the mellower season,
and what we lose in flowers,
we more than gain in fruits.

– Samuel Butler

5	6	7
Daylight Savings Ends		Election Day
12	13	14
19	20	21
26	27	28

October

S	M	T	W	T	F	S
	1	2	3	4	5	6	7
8	9	10	11	12	13	14
15	16	17	18	19	20	21
22	23	24	25	26	27	28
29	30	31				

December

S	M	T	W	T	F	S
					1	2
3	4	5	6	7	8	9
10	11	12	13	14	15	16
17	18	19	20	21	22	23
24/31	25	26	27	28	29	30

2023

Wednesday	Thursday	Friday	Saturday
1	2	3	4
8	9	10	11 Veterans' Day Remembrance Day (Canada)
15	16	17	18
22	23 Thanksgiving	24	25
29	30		

November

For buffets or dinner parties, save time by rolling up flatware in colorful napkins, tying with ribbon bows and stacking in a flat basket. Even kids can help!

1 Wednesday

2 Thursday

3 Friday

4 Saturday

5 Sunday

Daylight Savings Ends

November

Monday 6

Tuesday 7

Election Day

Wednesday 8

Thursday 9

Friday 10

Saturday 11

Veterans' Day
Remembrance Day
(Canada)

Sunday 12

November

13 _Monday_

14 _Tuesday_

15 _Wednesday_

16 _Thursday_

17 _Friday_

18 _Saturday_

19 _Sunday_

November

Monday 20

Tuesday 21

Wednesday 22

Thanksgiving   Thursday 23

Friday 24

Saturday 25

Sunday 26

November

27 Monday

28 Tuesday

29 Wednesday

30 Thursday

December

December

Notes	Sunday	Monday	Tuesday
	3	4	5
	10	11	12
	17	18	19
	24 / New Year's Eve 31	25 Christmas	26 Boxing Day (Canada)

November

S	M	T	W	T	F	S
			1	2	3	4
5	6	7	8	9	10	11
12	13	14	15	16	17	18
19	20	21	22	23	24	25
26	27	28	29	30		

January

S	M	T	W	T	F	S
	1	2	3	4	5	6
7	8	9	10	11	12	13
14	15	16	17	18	19	20
21	22	23	24	25	26	27
28	29	30	31			

2023

Wednesday	Thursday	Friday	Saturday
		1	2
6	7 Hanukkah (Sundown)	8	9
13	14	15	16
20	21 First Day of Winter	22	23
27	28	29	30

December

Mrs. Claus' Christmas Bread

1 c. sugar
2 T. butter, softened
1 egg, beaten
2 c. all-purpose flour
1 t. baking powder

1/2 t. baking soda
1/2 t. salt
3/4 c. orange juice
1 c. cranberries, chopped
1/2 c. chopped pecans

Blend sugar, butter and egg together in a large bowl. Add remaining ingredients; mix well and pour into a greased 9"x5" loaf pan. Bake at 350 degrees for 45 to 50 minutes. Makes one loaf.

1 Friday

2 Saturday

3 Sunday

December

Monday 4

Tuesday 5

Wednesday 6

Hanukkah (Sundown)

Thursday 7

Friday 8

Saturday 9

Sunday 10

December

11 Monday

12 Tuesday

13 Wednesday

14 Thursday

15 Friday

16 Saturday

17 Sunday

December

Monday 18

Tuesday 19

Wednesday 20

First Day of Winter   Thursday 21

Friday 22

Saturday 23

Sunday 24

December

25 Monday   Christmas

26 Tuesday   Boxing Day (Canada)

27 Wednesday

28 Thursday

29 Friday

30 Saturday

31 Sunday   New Year's Eve

December

Christmas Peppermint & Chocolate Meringues

2 egg whites
1/8 t. cream of tartar
1/8 t. salt
3/4 c. sugar
1/2 t. vanilla extract

3 T. peppermint candies, crushed
2 c. mini semi-sweet chocolate chips

In a large bowl, beat egg whites with an electric mixer at high speed until foamy. Add cream of tartar and salt, beating until mixed. Gradually add sugar, one tablespoon at a time, beating well after each addition until stiff peaks form. Gently fold in remaining ingredients. Drop by teaspoonfuls 1-1/2 inches apart on baking sheets sprayed with non-stick vegetable spray. Bake at 250 degrees for 40 minutes, or until dry. Remove to wire racks to cool completely. Store in an airtight container. Makes 3 dozen.

2023

January
S	M	T	W	T	F	S
	1	2	3	4	5	6	7
8	9	10	11	12	13	14
15	16	17	18	19	20	21
22	23	24	25	26	27	28
29	30	31

February
S	M	T	W	T	F	S
			1	2	3	4
5	6	7	8	9	10	11
12	13	14	15	16	17	18
19	20	21	22	23	24	25
26	27	28

March
S	M	T	W	T	F	S
			1	2	3	4
5	6	7	8	9	10	11
12	13	14	15	16	17	18
19	20	21	22	23	24	25
26	27	28	29	30	31

April
S	M	T	W	T	F	S
						1
2	3	4	5	6	7	8
9	10	11	12	13	14	15
16	17	18	19	20	21	22
23	24	25	26	27	28	29
30

May
S	M	T	W	T	F	S
	1	2	3	4	5	6
7	8	9	10	11	12	13
14	15	16	17	18	19	20
21	22	23	24	25	26	27
28	29	30	31

June
S	M	T	W	T	F	S
				1	2	3
4	5	6	7	8	9	10
11	12	13	14	15	16	17
18	19	20	21	22	23	24
25	26	27	28	29	30

July
S	M	T	W	T	F	S
						1
2	3	4	5	6	7	8
9	10	11	12	13	14	15
16	17	18	19	20	21	22
23	24	25	26	27	28	29
30	31

August
S	M	T	W	T	F	S
		1	2	3	4	5
6	7	8	9	10	11	12
13	14	15	16	17	18	19
20	21	22	23	24	25	26
27	28	29	30	31

September
S	M	T	W	T	F	S
					1	2
3	4	5	6	7	8	9
10	11	12	13	14	15	16
17	18	19	20	21	22	23
24	25	26	27	28	29	30

October
S	M	T	W	T	F	S
1	2	3	4	5	6	7
8	9	10	11	12	13	14
15	16	17	18	19	20	21
22	23	24	25	26	27	28
29	30	31

November
S	M	T	W	T	F	S
			1	2	3	4
5	6	7	8	9	10	11
12	13	14	15	16	17	18
19	20	21	22	23	24	25
26	27	28	29	30

December
S	M	T	W	T	F	S
					1	2
3	4	5	6	7	8	9
10	11	12	13	14	15	16
17	18	19	20	21	22	23
24	25	26	27	28	29	30
31

2024

January
S	M	T	W	T	F	S
	1	2	3	4	5	6
7	8	9	10	11	12	13
14	15	16	17	18	19	20
21	22	23	24	25	26	27
28	29	30	31

February
S	M	T	W	T	F	S
				1	2	3
4	5	6	7	8	9	10
11	12	13	14	15	16	17
18	19	20	21	22	23	24
25	26	27	28	29

March
S	M	T	W	T	F	S
					1	2
3	4	5	6	7	8	9
10	11	12	13	14	15	16
17	18	19	20	21	22	23
24	25	26	27	28	29	30
31

April
S	M	T	W	T	F	S
	1	2	3	4	5	6
7	8	9	10	11	12	13
14	15	16	17	18	19	20
21	22	23	24	25	26	27
28	29	30

May
S	M	T	W	T	F	S
			1	2	3	4
5	6	7	8	9	10	11
12	13	14	15	16	17	18
19	20	21	22	23	24	25
26	27	28	29	30	31

June
S	M	T	W	T	F	S
						1
2	3	4	5	6	7	8
9	10	11	12	13	14	15
16	17	18	19	20	21	22
23	24	25	26	27	28	29
30

July
S	M	T	W	T	F	S
	1	2	3	4	5	6
7	8	9	10	11	12	13
14	15	16	17	18	19	20
21	22	23	24	25	26	27
28	29	30	31

August
S	M	T	W	T	F	S
				1	2	3
4	5	6	7	8	9	10
11	12	13	14	15	16	17
18	19	20	21	22	23	24
25	26	27	28	29	30	31

September
S	M	T	W	T	F	S
1	2	3	4	5	6	7
8	9	10	11	12	13	14
15	16	17	18	19	20	21
22	23	24	25	26	27	28
29	30

October
S	M	T	W	T	F	S
		1	2	3	4	5
6	7	8	9	10	11	12
13	14	15	16	17	18	19
20	21	22	23	24	25	26
27	28	29	30	31

November
S	M	T	W	T	F	S
					1	2
3	4	5	6	7	8	9
10	11	12	13	14	15	16
17	18	19	20	21	22	23
24	25	26	27	28	29	30

December
S	M	T	W	T	F	S
1	2	3	4	5	6	7
8	9	10	11	12	13	14
15	16	17	18	19	20	21
22	23	24	25	26	27	28
29	30	31

Notes

Phone Numbers & Emergency Contacts

Phone Numbers & Emergency Contacts

Birthdays & Anniversaries

Birthdays &
Anniversaries

_____

_____

_____

_____

_____

_____

_____

_____

_____

_____

_____

_____

_____

_____

Gift List

Gift / Card